120 Solutions For Life

AVER STU

ISBN: 9781728785011

DEDICATION

I dedicate this book to someone special and dear to me. Someone who believed in me when I didn't believe in myself. Someone who inspired me to reach for my dreams and made me realize the potential within me which I never realized myself. Without this someone, I couldn't possibly have written this book. So, to this someone, thank you, for making this possible.

CONTENTS

ACKNOWLEDGMENTS

This book would not have been possible without the support of my readers. I am grateful to all of those with whom I have had the pleasure of getting to know throughout my journey as a writer. Each chapter of this book has been inspired by the daily struggles and challenges that my readers go through, and nothing has been more important to me in the pursuit of writing this book than helping my readers through the provision of my words of wisdom. Above all, I would like to thank everyone, whose love and guidance are with me in whatever I pursue in my life. I appreciate each and every one of my supporters and I feel blessed to have them root for me.

1) HAPPINESS IS A CHOICE

There isn't only one formula that the world should follow to find true happiness. There isn't one right way to be happy because what makes one person happy, might make another person sad. Happiness is a choice. Only you are responsible for how happy you are. Only you have the power to realize that you are in charge of your own happiness. You can't expect someone else to give you happiness, if you can't find it in yourself first. Happiness comes from within you, and the best thing about it is that it's a free choice.

2) ACCEPT YOURSELF

To accept yourself means to come to terms with yourself just the way you are, just the way you were born and the things about yourself that you cannot change. It means to have unconditional self-respect and self-love. You don't need to sit around waiting for the approval from other people because you should know that you are the only "you" there is, whether people choose to respect that or not. No one is perfect or ever will be, and that includes you, because everyone has flaws. Try to look at it this way: you're flawlessly flawful and imperfectly perfect, and that should be enough.

3 LOVE YOURSELF

Never make the mistake of failing to love yourself before loving someone else - because if you don't love yourself, how will you love them? To love yourself means to invest in your personal growth, to work on being the best version of you. Physically, mentally, spiritually and emotionally. You become a seed which you, yourself water on a daily basis in order to grow. The same principle applies when you want to love someone else – to keep the love strong, you would water it by giving them attention, care, respect, and so much more. But focus on doing all these things to yourself first. Love yourself first.

4 HEALTH IS IMPORTANT

Be it physical or mental health, but both are equally important. Every time you eat or drink, you are either feeding disease into your body or fighting it. The same goes for every time you think – you are either keeping your mind in control or out of control. So be good to yourself; eat well, sleep well and think well. Because if you don't function properly, how will those who love you enjoy you being around feeling sick? And if you really think about it, the greatest gift that you can give to your loved ones is a healthy you.

5 BELIEVE THAT YOU CAN

When you start to believe in yourself, then you can do anything. Never doubt your ability when it comes to wanting to achieve a certain goal or dream that you have. Because doubt causes anxiety, and anxiety causes stress, and stress puts you off from achieving. To be successful in achievement, means that you should believe in yourself by controlling your thoughts, emotions and reactions. Maintain a positive attitude; stop thinking that you can't and start believing that you can.

6 BE IN CONTROL

Your life depends on the decisions that you make and the actions that you take. It doesn't matter what situation your life is in, but your decisions matter. You will be held accountable and responsible for anything wrong that happens in your life or anything that feels like it's not heading towards the right direction — simply because your decisions were out of control.

7 DON'T STRESS

To not stress is always easier said than done but stressing out will cause you to stress out even more. And the worst way to deal with it is by avoiding or running away from the thing that is increasing your stress levels. But sometimes it takes more than shortcuts to eliminate stress. Sometimes you really have to get off your backside and take action to address the root cause of it, and try to fix it. Remember it's not stress that kills you, but your reaction to it that does.

8 DON'T BE ANXIOUS

You don't need to feel anxious and tired all the time by continuously living "somewhere else", thinking about the future, or what will happen next. Anxiety will not change anything about the next moment, but it will make it worse. Instead shift your energy and focus on the present. Keep calm and embrace every next moment one step at a time.

9 DON'T FEAR

Beneath all your fears, lies great opportunities. There will be scary moments in life and sometimes you just really need to find the courage to be able to face up to them. One of the greatest discoveries you can ever make, is to find that you can do what you were afraid you couldn't do.

10 FORGIVENESS

When you decide to forgive someone, you become free - you no longer become their prisoner. You no longer have to waste your energy holding anger and hatred towards them. Forgiveness may not change the past, but it will definitely enlarge the future. Without forgiveness, your life will be a constant, endless cycle of bitterness and resentment. So forgive others because you deserve to live in peace.

11 UNFORGIVENESS

The roots of unforgiveness can be very toxic. They can grow deep within you and convince you that you have been extremely wronged by someone, that they must be punished and that you cannot be happy until they have received their punishment. It gives you a longing to be paid back for the pain you have endured - but the truth is, only God can pay you back if you trust Him and forgive your enemies.

12 WHY ME?

You keep asking yourself "why does this always happen to me?" when something doesn't go as planned, or when something bad happens. You focus too much on the negative side of things. But the truth is that whatever makes you notice the bad things is not that they always happen, but they rarely happen. In fact if they always happened then you wouldn't even talk or complain about it because you'd be used to it. And if they do actually happen quite frequently, ask yourself if there's something you can do to change it or how you feel about it. At the end of the day only you are responsible for how you feel.

13 ANGER

Anger is a natural emotion but it does not do you any justice when you choose to be angry at someone. That's because anger builds more anger, and more anger builds hate. All this drains your energy and as a result, like Buddha says, not only will you be punished for your anger, but you will also be punished by your anger.

14 LETTING GO

Sometimes, holding on to something or someone does more destruction than letting go. Maybe it's not meant to be, or maybe it's not good for you like you think it is. Perhaps you have tried more than enough to make it work, so you come to a point where you feel like giving up. Giving up, knowing that you tried your best, then letting go - hoping for the best.

15 FRIENDSHIP

Life is never easy alone, you can never live alone and you can't always tell your parents everything. That's why a true friend can sometimes become your chosen family because you know they always have your back. In times of difficulty, they will be there for you. You can trust them because they proved why you should. You have so much in common and the conversations you have seem to never end, because you can talk for hours and hours. The connection is deep and the bond is unbreakable. And when you're separate from them, you know they're always with you in your heart. But true friendship is rare, so if you ever find a good friend, never take advantage of them. Never take a good friend for granted. Because the day you lose a good friend, is the day you lose a piece of your heart, a piece of your life.

16 LOVE

One day you will experience the love that you deserve. The romantic kind of love. The kind of love that you won't have to beg for. The kind of love that will come and find you. One day someone will complete your love story but until then, be patient. There is someone out there for everyone, including you. Have faith for true love for it will be a blessing to embrace, which will last just as long as your patience. But love doesn't always have to be associated with romance. You can spread love to those whom you care about (other than your partner) such as your family and friends. Love is a gift, an emotion, expression, the cure, the way of living.

17 CHANGE

Just like the seasons change, people also change, everything is always changing. And sometimes, people leave, things go wrong, but that doesn't mean your life ends. Life doesn't stop for you. You have to learn to adapt to the change and continue living. But most importantly, strive to change yourself – be the change that you wish to see in the world.

18 ADAPT

Sometimes change can make you feel miserable; you wish some things could always stay the same, but unfortunately, they can't. The only way to survive change is to adapt to change. See it as a process and always be ready to go along with it at your own pace. This might mean accepting something that's out of your control.

19 FIND SUPPORT

Admitting that we need help is hard sometimes, but when you take the time out to learn from other people on how they survived change, you'll be really surprised how positively they respond. The truth is there are more people that are keen to help you than you probably know; it's just a matter of you reaching out to them.

20 KINDNESS

Kindness is free and no amount of it, whether big or small, ever goes to waste. As the saying goes, kindness is like a language that even the deaf can hear and the blind can see. Be kind to people for no reason, without expecting kindness back. You never know how far your act of kindness can reach someone or make a difference to their life. Always be kind.

21 BE YOUR OWN HERO

You keep waiting for someone to save you from your darkness, your troubles, your insecurities, or whatever it may be. But the truth is that you need to be the hero of your own life. It makes sense, because the person with the most power of your life is the same person who stares back at you every time you look in the mirror. You're responsible for your own decisions, thoughts, words and actions. And since you're always making mistakes, one of the biggest mistake that you can ever make is choosing to give the power of being saved, to someone else.

22 SELF-ACCEPTANCE

The heart of self-acceptance is to value yourself as a person no matter what and accepting that being a human being who messes up from time to time is okay. If you fail at something, it doesn't define you as a total failure. If you act stupidly, it doesn't define you as a stupid person. Self-acceptance simply differentiates between who you are and your behavior.

23 LIFE GROWS YOU

You might have gone through a lot that makes you believe your life will always be difficult. But you've been through it, you managed to do so and somehow it has shaped you into the person you've become today. Life doesn't always get easier, but it gets better. The more you go through life, the more you will also grow through life. You will also, one day, outgrow life – so keep on fighting and never give up.

24 BE LIKE THE SUN

Be like the sun that sets light across the earth. The sun that even after the end of the darkest night, you still decide to rise every morning. The sun that is so strong, that no one will be able to stop you from doing what you were always meant to do — shine.

25 YOU ARE BLESSED

You will experience a lot of downfalls along your journey but when you see others struggling with something such as poverty or an illness, you realize not to take your own status for granted. You realize that such a moment is when you accept how blessed you truly are because there are people around the world that have it much worse than you.

26 BEYOND BLESSINGS

You are blessed, sometimes a lot more than others, and sometimes a lot less, in different ways. Deep inside, you may feel that you are not blessed 'enough'. But have you ever once considered that what if what you feel you don't have is a blessing in itself? A blessing in disguise? These lack of blessings that you feel, they might actually be a trial for bigger blessings to come. So maybe you just need to be a little bit more patient because one day, you will experience blessings that are beyond your imagination.

27 KEEP GOING

Accept that what's done is done, and what's gone is gone. It might be difficult to move on but you have to keep going. And never look back, unless you want to see how far you've come. But regardless of that, keep going. Keep moving forward.

28 RELAX

You're not going to have your whole life planned out in one day. Just relax. Make realistic plans, goals and targets. Then just try to keep working towards them every day without fail. Everything will be okay.

29 PAIN ENDS

Always remember that pain does not enter your life for no reason. Look at it as a sign that means it will change you and your life, for the better. If pain can come, then pain can also go. So please never lose hope – hold on, pain ends.

30 RIGHT PERSON

Stop looking for the right person and start focusing on being the right person first. Once you master doing that, the right person will come along at the correct timing.

31 RESTFUL MIND

Keep your mind open, rather than narrow, because when you do, there is space to see things from different angles, and space to let things just be. You become more understanding of others. You notice more. You make the time to listen and to smile. You simply invite and attract good vibes. With a restful mind you can accomplish so much good things.

32 TEMPORARY

Everything in life is temporary. People don't stay forever, they leave. Pain doesn't last forever, it fades. Feelings don't stay the same, they change. We won't live forever, someday we will die. And so on. When you accept that life is temporary, you will live life to the fullest in every moment. You will be ready for whatever life throws at you because you'll know that nothing coming your way will stay forever. Life is simply too short. Nothing lasts forever. Here today, gone tomorrow. Everything is just temporary; nothing more, nothing less.

33 START AFRESH

Let go of the outer world and keep your mind focused on your inner reality. Connect all your thoughts, awareness and energy to your spiritual being. When you do so you will experience an incredible power of peace and light activate you. So just let it heal, refresh and finish the effects of the past and old memories. You will notice a great feeling of purity and cleansing fill you. It will make you feel fresher and stronger, as if you were born again.

34 SATISFACTION

To attain maximum satisfaction, you need to think about what makes you feel alive physically, mentally and spiritually. Satisfaction can only, truly come from you and only you. Nobody else.

35 BEAUTY

There are two kinds of beauty: one is of the soul and the other is of the body. Beauty can be seen in a soul which displays intelligence, good character, mannerisms, respect, many qualities which may exist in what shallow people would describe as an "ugly" person. And physical beauty is displayed by the body through someone's physical attributes such as their eyes, hair and posture. If you find that you are too concerned with looks, get to know someone first. After a while, when you've known someone, sometimes you forget about their physical appearance because you're attracted so much by the beauty of their soul and heart. The things that really matter, the things that last forever.

36 YOU'RE WORTH IT

Never lose your self-worth by searching for it in other people. When you know your worth, you'll stop trying to please others. Be with those who know your worth, for they will appreciate you for who you are.

37 YOU ARE BEAUTIFUL

You're beautiful because you're kind. You're beautiful because you're understanding. You're beautiful because you try. You're beautiful because you're full of love. You're beautiful because you're strong. You're beautiful because you take risks. You're beautiful because you're brave. You're beautiful because you never give up. You're beautiful because of your flaws. You're beautiful because you're you. And the list can go on forever! There are so many things that make you beautiful. You're just simply beautiful and you shouldn't wait for someone else to tell you that. You already know it, just take the time to see it.

38 BE YOU

If you can't be yourself, then you can never be happy. No one is you or can ever be you, and that is your real power. You may be insecure of showing something to the world, and you may have your own personal reasons for that which is fine. But if you try to take small steps in uncovering the 'real you' by giving it full expression, then it could make a huge difference to your happiness because when you are you, you are free. And when you are free, you are happy.

39 IT'S OKAY TO SAY NO

Sometimes saying no can be challenging because maybe you don't want to upset or disappoint someone. But remember, no matter what the situation is, you have a choice. You have a choice to say no without explaining yourself. Saying no can sometimes be the ultimate self-care.

40 KNOWLEDGE

Knowing too much is never enough because there is no limit to knowledge. But the more you seek it and the more you apply it, then the more you will elevate from it. Knowledge is power.

41 SCREWED UP

When you realize you screw up, you'll feel really bad about it. You feel genuine remorse and regret because you know that you have made a mistake, and that's normal. But don't beat yourself up for it. Everyone screws up sometimes. No one is perfect.

42 GO WITH THE FLOW

Accept that 'it is what it is' and you'll be okay. Once you've accepted that then you will learn to accept everything that life throws at you. Go with the flow, but never stop learning and striving to improve for the better. Just accept that whatever happens, will happen for the best.

43 WHY WORRY?

Problems, disappointments and uncertainties are all a part of life. Everyone has them. You should naturally expect them, so to think about them is necessary. But to worry about them is another thing, because it does no good. Worrying is easier to do than thinking and working constructively to approach your problems, but it is destructive because it can emotionally drain you. Stop worrying.

44 TEARS

Tears actually heal; emotional tears remove chemicals that have been built up during times of stress and difficulty. Animals produce tears that simply run from their eyes, but it is only us humans that produce emotional tears that remove toxic substances. So, tears do help your body. But more importantly, your tears are simply a reflection of how your heart speaks when your lips can't describe how much you've been hurt. Never be ashamed of your tears, because your tears symbolize your strength, not weakness.

45 MASKS

You don't need to wear hundreds of masks just because you want to fit in and be accepted by people. Drop the masks for once and be genuine. Without the masks, you're at your truest and authentic form. You're less fake and more free. This way you will attract all the right people, especially the ones who are meant to love and adore you for who you are without all the masks involved.

46 GOALS

Set some goals in your life and do whatever it takes to achieve them. Just don't focus too much on what will happen in the next week, month or year. But focus on right now, this moment, and do what you can to get closer to where you wish to be.

47 PAST MISTAKES

Leave your past mistakes where they belong - in the past! Don't think too much about them. They should teach you how to create a better future for yourself, not cause you to be scared of it. Don't be defined by your past mistakes, be guided by them.

48 TAKE NEW CHANCES

You're too comfortable with what you already have and maybe you have settled for it. But why not give yourself a chance to try new things? Get out of your comfort zone more often and be open to chances (because maybe you deserve better). You never know, sometimes they can be life-changing.

49 THOUGHTS

Make time for thoughts. Give yourself some time and space to think, question, reflect and ponder upon life. Your thoughts shape you and can change your world. Always keep them positive.

50 FOLLOW YOUR DREAMS

If you can dream about it then nothing can stop you from achieving it. Don't give up on your dreams just because you think it's too much hard work or time consuming – remember if you can't stop thinking about it, don't stop working for it. Ultimately you can turn your dreams into reality, if you try your best.

51 DEALING WITH PROBLEMS

When you face problems in life, don't avoid them or leave them to solve by themselves. That's probably the worst way to approach problems. The best way would be to consider three solutions: change the situation, change how you interpret it, or change your response to it. So even if the first solution is not possible, the other two always are. Problems can get solved, but only if you permit.

52 CHALLENGES

When life throws challenges at you, don't see them just as challenges. See them as motivation. Let them motivate you to change and see who you can become. Often, challenges will make your life more interesting and meaningful.

53 DIFFICULT PEOPLE

Difficult people will exist in all areas of your life. You can't change a difficult person because usually they are quite happy to be as they are. So if you can't change them, you need to deal with them by not letting them manipulate you. Do not allow them to have a negative effect on your own emotions, mood and behavior.

54 LESSONS

When people try to tell you about their life experiences, you will never understand them until you go through them yourself first. But yes, it's always good to learn from other people's mistakes since you don't have all the time in the world to commit every mistake possible. Still, be thankful for your experiences. They help you learn and grow. They are what ultimately shape you as a person.

55 REGRETS

When you have feelings of regrets towards something that you may have or have not done, or have had happened to you, don't let it consume your life. Instead, accept the regrets as lessons learned. But never regret something that once made you happy or smile, because at that time it was exactly what you wanted. For future reference though, keep in mind that regrets may last forever – so if you have an opportunity to do something new, take it. If you want to tell someone about your feelings, tell them. If you want to travel, do it. Whatever you want to do, take action now. Don't live the rest of your life regretting all the chances that you didn't take.

56 EMOTIONS

Emotions are an essential part of life but be careful not to be completely controlled by them. Emotions come and go. Always be grateful for your emotions as they enable you to connect with people, teach you valuable life lessons and enrich your life experiences. You are not defined by your emotions, but don't ignore them – rather, embrace them and then let them drift away.

57 FEELINGS

There is nothing wrong with expressing or sharing your feelings as long as it is not negative or aggressive. You will never lose those who truly matter to you because they respect and value your emotions. But disguising your feelings or emotions only ends up hurting you. It causes a build-up of stress as you turn your feelings in on yourself rather than dealing with them. Try to be more open about your feelings because if you don't then you will cause problems for yourself.

58 SELF-CRITICISM

When you learn how to reduce self-criticism and improve yourself, it will be difficult for other people's words and actions to harm you. When you learn to understand yourself better, you begin to understand others too. You will begin to see something that has made others the way that they are. And once you begin to empathise with someone, no matter how bad or dreadful of a person they may be, they won't have the power to harm you.

59 HURT

Throughout your life some people will hurt you, or at least try to. But when they do so, don't hurt them back because that would mean you're only just as bad as they are. They're already hurtful, so don't become like them because you are way better than this. Choose to forgive them. It might still hurt, but it will hurt them even more when they see that you've released yourself from their control. Sometimes such people will hurt you only to happily see you suffer. Do not give them that advantage. Just try to ignore them, forgive them and move on because you deserve peace. Maybe one day, someone will hurt them just the way that they hurt you, and that will be the day when they will realize their mistake and feel bad for hurting you.

60 NEW DAY

Every day is a new beginning to start afresh, with a new hope that it will be better than yesterday. So leave the bad memories of yesterday behind, live today to the fullest, and have faith for a better tomorrow.

61 HATERS

No matter how good you are as a person, there's always going to be someone against you. Someone who will criticize you and try to bring you down. But don't let a hater be the reason why you stop moving forward. Don't let them be the limit of your success and the life that you have always dreamed of living.

62 TRUST

Trusting people has become hard nowadays because they abuse or violate its meaning. To trust, is the easiest thing to do. But it's really difficult to gain back because once someone breaks your trust, then it feels impossible to rebuild it. Don't trust people too easily. Sometimes they are not always what they seem. Let them earn your trust first, but don't freely give it out if they don't deserve it. Of course, when someone decides to trust you, respect them, because sometimes it takes a lot of courage to put trust out there. Treat people's trust preciously, just like how you'd want people to treat yours.

63 TIME

Time waits for no one; the clock is always ticking. And just like the time, you must also learn to do the same thing. Keep ticking forward.

64 EGO

Ego only destroys relationships. People let ego hold them back from saying some of the most important words in life such as "I miss you" and "I am sorry". When you're in a situation where you feel you should handle something difficult, try to be the bigger person - let your ego fade and do/say what you have to. This way you will feel more complete, because anything left unsaid or undone will only feed your ego and disturb the peace of your soul.

65 EXPECTATIONS

When you expect highly of someone or a situation, you'll end up feeling disappointed. Expectations will only frustrate you because they make you feel like you need to control the outcome of things, when really you don't have the power to do so. The only control that you have power over is your expectations – let go of them. The best way to avoid disappointment is to simply not expect anything from anyone.

66 APPRECIATE YOUR PARENTS

A lot of people spend so much of their time wishing that their parents would leave them alone, only to realize that their parents are the ones who have always been there and provided for them. No matter what, love and appreciate your parents because you never know what they went through or sacrificed just to protect you.

67 GOD

True peace comes from knowing that God exists. Put your trust in God and His plans for you. The more you rely on God, the more you'll accept that He is truly reliable. You'll realize just how unconditional His love is for you. You'll realize that God is enough.

68 GOD KNOWS

God knows everything. God knows about every sin that we will commit before we commit it. He does not expect us to be perfect or to never make mistakes. In fact, God is never surprised when we make mistakes; the truth is that He has already decided to be merciful and forgiving. But what God does expect for us is to love Him, worship Him, ask for forgiveness and want His will. He just wants us to be quick to repent and become spiritually stronger for His sake, and for our well-being.

69 SPIRITUALITY

It doesn't matter how happy you are, but if there's a lack of spirituality within you then there is always going to be a 'hole'. There are many definitions of spirituality but most of it is to do with your sense of connection with other things, including from people you know, with people you don't know, animals, plants, to the furthest reaches of the universe. The question is, if you knew there were human beings living on another planet, would it make any difference to you? If it would, then that's spirituality. Spirituality is the sense that you're connected to life, even though no actual connection is clearly evident.

70 PRAY

Prayer is powerful. It is simply a conversation between you and God where you pray in times of need and in times where you thank God for everything in your life. By praying, you leave your worries, troubles and even happiness in the hands of the Creator who just listens and responds by making unique plans for you. Prayer can solve all your problems so don't underestimate the power of a single call to God. It can literally turn your whole life around.

71 REPENT

Once you admit that you're a sinner, you must repent of your sins. This means that you're not only deeply sorry for your sins, but you're willing to stop doing them. Living the rest of your life in sin is a low level of life, but when you repent, you are giving yourself the chance to return to the highest place that God desires for you.

72 FATE

The road of life will sometimes take an unexpected turn and you will have no option other than to follow it, only to end up in the place you are supposed to be. This is called fate, which you can't control. Learn to accept the things to which fate attaches you, and do so with all your heart.

73 MIRACLES

The most incredible thing about miracles is that they happen. But whether you experience miracles or not, depends on how you choose to view them. The truth is, miracles happen every day – and, to be able to wake up to a new day is a miracle in itself. If you try to change your perspective of what a miracle is, you'll see them all around you.

74 GIVING

Giving is one of the best actions you can make towards achieving genuine happiness. True giving comes from the heart, without expecting anything in return. You'll find that the more you give, the more you'll receive. So if you ever feel unhappy then try making someone else happy and see what happens. The power of giving is that it feels good, because you give to others unselfishly with pure kindness and generosity.

75 WORDS

We live and breathe words. They are powerful, they have the ability to create a moment and equally have the strength to destroy it. Words have the power to build people up or break them down. You must choose your words carefully before you voice them to others - but most importantly, the words that you voice to yourself will either make you or break you as a person. Always keep your words positive.

76 RELATIONSHIPS

You know it's a true relationship when you are free to be yourself – to laugh with them, never at them; to cry with them, never because of them; to love them, and to love being loved. Such a relationship is based upon freedom and can never grow in a heart that is empty. But not every relationship is perfect or will provide happiness every day – the only way of developing through them is by surviving through the difficult times together, and simply being there for each other no matter what.

77 COMMUNICATION IS KEY

Any satisfying kind of relationship, whether it is with your family, friends or even partner, requires good communication and mutual understanding. If there is none of this and you end up disagreeing or having an argument, then you typically stop talking to each other. You need to get over this barrier and start communicating – listen carefully and express how you feel. If you don't want to lose those who are dear to you then don't risk the lack of communication, because it is the foundation of what keeps you close together.

78 SOLITUDE

Being comfortably alone is when you feel like you don't have to answer anybody, you just do what you want, alone. That's solitude, which is strength; and to depend on the presence of the crowd is weakness. The reality is that you're only lonely if you're not there for you. So embrace all the times that you have alone because that's when you are likely to restore and understand yourself more than anything else.

79 ATTITUDE

Attitude is a state of mind which depends on the actions you take in life. A right attitude can take you to places while a wrong attitude can leave you in the dumps. It determines how you experience every part of your life, so be sure to have a positive one.

80 GRATITUDE

Gratitude is all about realizing that there is a source of goodness which is outside of ourselves. Start counting your blessings, be thankful for everything, appreciate simple pleasures and everything that you receive. Don't forget to give thanks to those around you, it will make both you and them happier.

81 DEATH

If anything is certain in life, then it is death. No one can avoid or run away from it. It can hit you during any moment without warning. So really, it's pointless to have obsessive thoughts about death because such thoughts are what only stop you from living the life you wish to live. You can stop this. From now and onwards concentrate on what's important in life. Strive to make every day count; work towards your dreams and goals, be a kind, generous and loving person, and do what makes you happy. And be sure to live each day of your life like it is the last day of your life.

82 KEEP SMILING

One smile can make all the difference in the world. It has the power to release stress, calm you down, make you attractive, make someone else happy and believe it or not, smiling can actually cause happiness. Never stop smiling because you never know how much of a positive impact your smile can have on yourself and those around you.

83 LIFE IS A JOURNEY

Life is a journey because you will go through different experiences. But regardless of whatever you go through, learn to grow through it. Whenever you feel like life is attacking you, see it as an opportunity to help you with your growth.

84 COMPETITION

Life is not a competition. It's not about who finishes what first, or who has the best of everything, or even who is better than who else. When you compete against other people, you'll always lose because everyone is different. Learn to compete against the person you were last year, last month, yesterday, or even just a few minutes ago. Be in a constant battle to better yourself from the past. That is real competition, and that is what will shape you into becoming a real winner.

85 POSITIVE THINKING

Don't be someone who focuses on what's impossible so much that all they see is impossibility. Don't be negative. Be someone who tries to think positive in every situation. Think about what's possible, because when you concentrate on the possibilities, they make things happen.

86 PUSH OUT FEELINGS

Get rid of all the feelings that aren't positive. Don't let negative thoughts and feelings control you when you're feeling low. Your best bet is to push your negative feelings aside and only focus on the positive things in your life.

87 SUCCESS

If you know that you want to succeed, then you will know what it takes to succeed. Success is always a process; there will be good days as well as bad days. No one in life has ever made it big with success by going through an easy, challenge-free path to their victory. If you learn to embrace the process of success including all the challenges that come with it, then you will achieve your own victory with more ease. You will become successful.

88 MAKE GOALS

A sense of purpose is a fundamental human need because without purpose or meaning in your life, you become lost. But with goals, you become aware of the path that you have to follow in order to get there – and you have something to aim at. Achieving your goals will take commitment, time and effort – but only with a realistic and manageable planned route. So make a start now and everything else will gradually fall into place.

89 FAILURE

You will encounter many failures throughout your life, but just because you do, it doesn't mean that you are automatically defined as a failure. Everyone fails at something, and in every success story you will learn that someone fell down countless times – yet they still chose to get back up and continue to walk through their journey of success. So don't give up. Keep trying. Try and try again, until you succeed. Real failure is when you stop trying.

90 SELF-DOUBT

Self-doubt is real because everyone has it. Gaining confidence and losing confidence is real too. But in the end, it all comes down to how much you let doubt take control over your life. Sometimes doubt can completely drown you, making you feel insecure and fearful of what's coming next. Don't let that happen. Instead, let doubt motivate you to clear out any blocks within yourself, become fearless and ready to tackle the unknown.

91 NEVER GIVE UP

You will hear about other people becoming really successful and wonder why you're not like them. But what you may not know is that it took them a huge amount of hard work and effort to get where they are. It wasn't easy for them, and most likely you probably feel that your own journey towards success isn't easy either. But they proved it's possible - and if they can do it, then you can too. So don't give up, keep working hard and soon enough you'll even become a great success yourself.

92 YOUR LIFE IS A CHOICE

Life will present you with many decisions to make, many journeys to go through and many lessons to learn from. But in the end, it depends upon how you choose to take it all. Life is simply a matter of choices, and whatever choice you make, ultimately makes you. Some choices you'll regret, some choices you'll be proud of, and some choices which will haunt you forever. The main point is that you are what you choose to be. So be responsible for your life and choose to make it amazing.

93 TAKE RISKS

To risk nothing, is to risk everything. Learn to take risks because if you don't, then how else will you move forward in life? How else will you learn from your mistakes? If you're not taking risks simply because of failure, then you need to stop thinking like that. There is no such thing as failure – only successes and learning experiences.

94 SIMPLICITY

Simplicity is like focusing on that which is important and letting go of everything else. It can mean living with less and still being happy, but more so, it can be seen as an attitude or an approach to life. Simplicity will allow you to achieve more of what truly matters, e.g. f you're engaged in a task or conversation with an attitude of simplicity then you would be willing to keep yourself focused on the main topic rather than getting lost in a clutter of distractions. If you choose to live simply, you will discover that your life becomes less stressful and less complicated.

95 COMPLIMENTS

Compliments cost nothing and have the power to make someone's day. Get into the habit of giving compliments to those around you - don't save them just for special occasions. By complimenting others, you will bring happiness and a sense of belonging into their lives.

96 EXPRESS YOURSELF

Anything that you do to express yourself is a form of art. Do something that reflects who you are, something that you're capable of doing, something that you love doing or something that you really care about. Once you believe in your ability to do something that will express who you are as an individual, you will feel free.

97 CONTENTMENT

Contentment involves being happy when you don't have everything. This feeling of contentment doesn't depend on what you have but it depends on how you feel. Learn to be content, because it's a sure way of enjoying what you already have, rather than wishing for things that you don't have.

98 THE MIRROR

The mirror can tell you a lot about the outside of your body but that's not what mostly defines your beauty. What the mirror doesn't tell you is about the inside of your body including all its amazing functions, or that you and your body are the most brilliant creations of the universe.

99 MONEY

Most people spend their entire lives working towards money: they think about making more, getting more, keeping more and spending more. It's true that money is necessary for the basics of life or to enjoy some of the finer things, but you should never have to think that increasing money means increasing your happiness – it just causes your desire for more money.

100 BE OPEN

Each day that you wake up to holds a surprise - you just have to open up your mind to allow the opportunity to experience what comes your way. Be open to new ideas and change and learn to embrace it all. Thinking with an open mind will give you the option of creating positivity and stronger results for your life.

101 EXERCISE

Exercise is not only important for your health, but it is also important for how you feel about yourself. When you get stronger, eat better and live healthier, you automatically begin to feel like a whole new different and improved person.

102 MINDSET

Your mind is a powerful thing; when you fill it with positive thoughts, you begin to notice positive results and changes to your life. When it changes, everything on the outside will change along with it too. Mindset is all about realizing your negative habits, then replacing them with positive ones. It's all about training your mind to see your true potential. A good mindset will ultimately help you focus on maintaining good habits.

103 INSPIRE

Being able to inspire others is something you should aspire to do. There is nothing more rewarding than encouraging your friends, family, or your followers to achieve great and wonderful things in life. So be honest about who you are and your own shortcomings and failures. People are more likely to follow and be inspired by someone who is a real human being, than by someone who seems too good to be true.

104 SOCIAL MEDIA

Social media changes the way that we communicate and the way that we are perceived, both positively and negatively. There are lots of pros and cons about social media but it just depends on how you choose to handle it and connect with others. If used correctly, social media can really expand your universe.

105 THE NEWS

Don't be too obsessed with the news. Sometimes the news is consumed by all kinds of depressing information. If you're already having a bad day or if your mood is switched off, then skip the news for the day and instead do something that gives you joy.

106 BOREDOM

Being bored tends to turn your mind inward and encourages reflection. When you're rushing about, there's no time to think. But when you're bored, there's nothing else to do other than think. Use boredom as an opportunity to see it as a sign that you need to reflect upon yourself and change for the better. Sometimes it might mean that you need rest, or other times it might mean that you need to get creative.

107 THEIR APPROVAL

When you seek the approval of other people, you believe that it matters what they think. But the truth is that it matters what you think. Far too many of us fall into this kind of trap. Confidence is a big part of it which is hard to find when you rely on the opinion of others to determine your success and achievements. You need to find that confidence and be able to judge your own actions for yourself. Once you master how to do this, you will feel comfortable with yourself even during the most difficult times.

108 DON'T LET THEM BULLY YOU

Bullies are the people who usually need you to feel inferior and afraid just so that they could feel more powerful. Their so-called self-value comes from taking away yours, but don't let them have this power over you. Just define yourself completely with no care in what they think of you because the truth is that they have nothing better to do. They truly are much weaker than you think.

109 CAREER

There is more to life than your career. There are people such as your friends and family who make your life worthwhile. If you completely devote yourself into a high-pressure career for too long then you'll find that all of those important people will drift away. But you don't have to give up your career; you just have to do something that you enjoy, and something that allows you to be flexible with your time. Just make sure that it allows you to live a proper life too.

110 FOLLOW YOUR PASSION

When you take the time to follow your interest in life it means that you are advancing your talent and you will be able to feel good about yourself. You will get the feeling of happiness and fulfilment. Also, it is important to follow your passion because when you do so, you are tapping into the real you where you will begin to find out about your truly amazing talents.

111 TRAVEL

Sometimes you need to travel simply because you deserve a break. It gives you the chance to disconnect from your daily life and let go of your responsibilities for a moment only to focus on yourself. Travel as much as you can because it will help you experience new things and open up your mind to the outside world. When you return home you'll feel more energized, like your balance has been restored, and you can return back to your normal routine with a refreshed mindset.

112 EXCUSES

Don't let your excuses be the reason why you fail to progress in your dreams and goals because the more you make excuses, the more comfortable you get with settling for average or maybe even less than that – and be honest with yourself, do you really want that? Of course not. Start believing in yourself that you are destined for greatness. Take small steps to overcome your limitations, and then you will find that it becomes easier to stay focused. Your excuses should no longer distract you, because you're too focused on being successful.

113 BE A READER

Unlike magazines, internet posts or e-mails that don't hold a large amount of information, books are different; they tell the whole story through many chapters. By reading more books, you will be able to discover new ideas, concepts, places and people, all of which have the power to improve your thinking process. Not only that, but books will also give you a positive outlook towards life. Successful people read daily and consistently, so get yourself into the habit of doing that too.

114 YOUR LIFE IS A CHOICE

Everything that has ever happened to you, reflects on the series of choices that you made. Your choices brought you to this moment. When you understand that your choices are important and that they guide you and shape you – then you're giving yourself the opportunity to accept life's outcomes and to be in control of the future that you want.

115 LOOK UP

You must look up, look ahead and keep setting yourself goals, dreams and ambitions. Believe that you are capable of achieving anything and remember that good isn't good enough — you can always do better than that. Always set yourself high standards.

116 YOUR DREAMS HAVE NO DEADLINE

It doesn't matter who you are as a person whether it's your age, background, past, or current life situation — but you still have the power to make your dreams come true. Nothing or no one can stop that except for you because you are your only limit. You are the one who sees your dreams, so only you can control whether you will accomplish them or not. Remember, it's never too early or too late to turn your dreams into reality so go and do something today that will take you a step closer towards them.

117 KEEP LEARNING

When you learn from experiences of pain, you end up seeing life differently. Learning is a process of gaining knowledge through experiences. In the learning process, your pain typically exists to help strengthen you as a person. Don't ignore your pain. Pay attention to it carefully because it might be trying to teach you something. The more you learn, the more knowledge you gain, and that is what gives life meaning.

118 REMEMBER

No matter how bad things get, always remember that they could be much worse. Try to appreciate all the good things that are already in your life, even when it seems like the bad outweighs the good. Because the more you appreciate the good things, the less you will focus on the bad things, and the more you will be blessed with greater things. Always remember that.

119 CHANGE YOUR VIBE

It's true, what you put out into the universe is what you will get back. So stop putting out bad energy and practice more positivity. This attracts good things to gravitate towards you. And whether it works or not, it doesn't really matter because you'll feel much better about yourself either way.

120 DO IT NOW

Life will give you endless opportunities to succeed and if you're not going to tell yourself 'do it now', then you're going to miss out. So starting from today, start responding 'yes' to every opportunity that life offers you. If you feel strongly about doing something then don't wait for the 'right time' – do it now!

~END OF BOOK~

ABOUT THE AUTHOR

Aver Stu is a student and entrepreneur based in England, UK, who has always had a passion for reading and writing, and enjoys blogging her content (of inspirational life quotes and sayings) on different social media platforms;

Instagram.com/average__student

Twitter.com/aver_stu

Pinterest.com/averstu

Weheartit.com/averstu

She also has her own website where her content is organized at:

averstu.com

If you have any queries or simply wish to contact Aver, please do so via her website contact page and she will respond back to you as soon as possible. Thank you.